How to Crochet Corner 2 Corner and Ripple Afghans

Popular and Timeless Techniques for You to Learn

By Dorothy Wilks

Hello and thank you for purchasing this book. In this book we will learn two of the most popular afghan techniques. One is relatively new, the Corner 2 Corner or C2C pattern, and the timeless ripple or wave stitch. Both of these patterns create beautiful works of art which are sure to become treasured family heirlooms. Once you understand these techniques you can stitch up afghans and throws of all sizes to keep or give away to lucky recipients. These techniques are perfect for the novice or advanced crochet enthusiast. If you're a beginner you only need to know the basic stitches to learn both of these techniques. More advanced crochet artists will appreciate the flexibility and variety these techniques offer. So if you're ready let's get busy and learn these two fun and exciting techniques.

Contents

Stitches and Techniques You Need to Know

You only need to master basic crochet stitches to be able to make both a C2C and ripple afghan or throw. In this chapter I will review how to crochet a chain, single crochet, double crochet, half double crochet, treble crochet, cluster stitches, and shell stitches. Like all crochet projects it is how you combine these basic stitches which create the desired technique.

Chain Stitches

You will use chain stitches to create a foundation chain for a ripple afghan and to start a new square in the C2C pattern. First make a slip knot and place it on your hook. Next place the yarn over your hook and draw it through the loop on the hook. This is the first chain stitch. Yarn over and pull through the loop on your hook to create the next chain stitch and repeat until you have the correct number of chain stitches called for in your pattern. You do not count the loop on your hook as a chain stitch when counting your stitches.

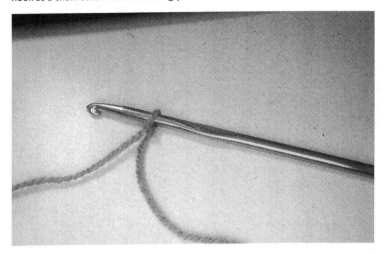

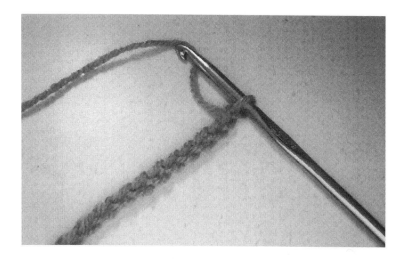

Turning Chain

When you reach the end of a row you will have to chain the appropriate number of stitches to count for the first stitch in the row. For single crochet you chain one, half double crochet you chain two, double crochet you chain three, and treble crochet you chain four or five. The next stitch is not done into the base of the turning chain, but in the stitch next to it. When you reach the end of the row you will work the last stitch into the last chain of the turning chain catching two loops on the top of your hook.

For example if you are using double crochet when you reach the end of the row the last double crochet stitch is worked into the third turning chain. This is why it is important to count your stitches. Your sides may become uneven or your rows may increase or decrease if you do not work the last stitch in the correct place.

Single Crochet

Using your chain insert the hook into the second chain stitch from your hook. Yarn over and pull through. You will now have two loops on the hook. Yarn over and pull through both loops at once. To crochet the next single crochet stitch insert the hook into the next chain stitch, yarn over and pull through, yarn over and pull through both loops on your hook. When you reach the end of the row and turn your work chain one and insert the hook into the first stitch away from your hook. Unless otherwise specified you do not insert the hook directly below the first chain stitch of the new row. Also the first chain one counts as the first stitch unless specified by the pattern.

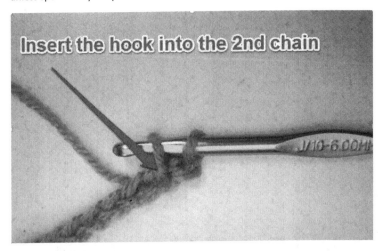

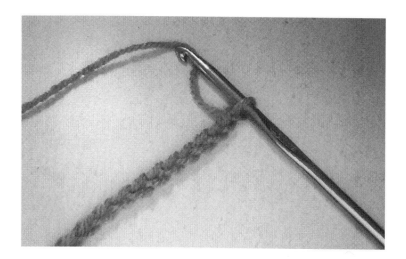

Turning Chain

When you reach the end of a row you will have to chain the appropriate number of stitches to count for the first stitch in the row. For single crochet you chain one, half double crochet you chain two, double crochet you chain three, and treble crochet you chain four or five. The next stitch is not done into the base of the turning chain, but in the stitch next to it. When you reach the end of the row you will work the last stitch into the last chain of the turning chain catching two loops on the top of your hook.

For example if you are using double crochet when you reach the end of the row the last double crochet stitch is worked into the third turning chain. This is why it is important to count your stitches. Your sides may become uneven or your rows may increase or decrease if you do not work the last stitch in the correct place.

Single Crochet

Using your chain insert the hook into the second chain stitch from your hook. Yarn over and pull through. You will now have two loops on the hook. Yarn over and pull through both loops at once. To crochet the next single crochet stitch insert the hook into the next chain stitch, yarn over and pull through, yarn over and pull through both loops on your hook. When you reach the end of the row and turn your work chain one and insert the hook into the first stitch away from your hook. Unless otherwise specified you do not insert the hook directly below the first chain stitch of the new row. Also the first chain one counts as the first stitch unless specified by the pattern.

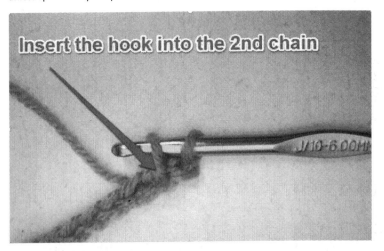

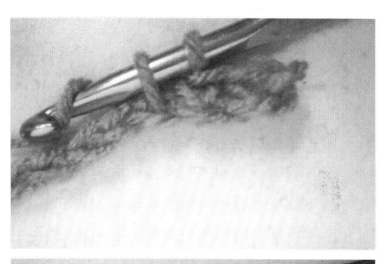

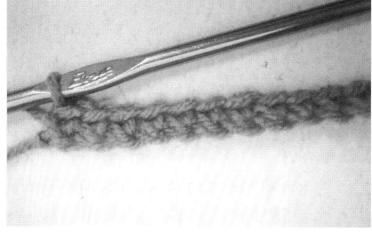

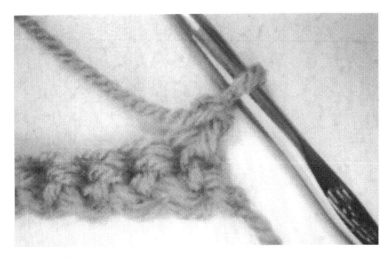

Double Crochet

The double crochet stitch is used a lot in many patterns. Before you insert the hook into the next stitch yarn over and then insert the hook and yarn over again. Pull through and you will have three loops on your hook. Yarn over and pull through the first two loops. Yarn over and pull through the last two loops.

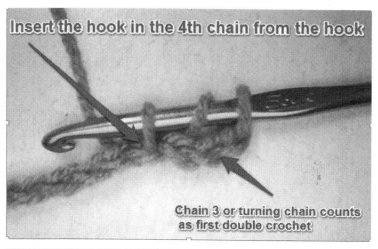

Insert the hook in the 4th chain from the hook

Chain 3 or turning chain counts as first double crochet

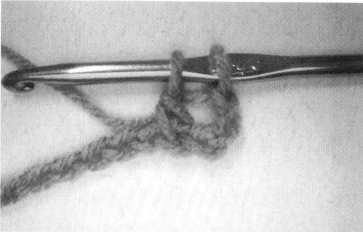

When you start a new row you will again chain three and count it as the first double crochet stitch.

At the end of the row the last stitch goes into the last chain stitch of the starting chain. Be sure to catch two loops on your hook so the stitch will be secure and not stretch out.

Treble or Triple Crochet

The treble (also known as the triple) crochet creates height in a pattern. Before you insert the hook into the next stitch yarn over twice and then insert the hook. Yarn over once and pull through the stitch. You will now have four loops on the hook. Yarn over and pull through two loops on the hook three times. You will notice how much higher the treble crochet stitch is than the other stitches.

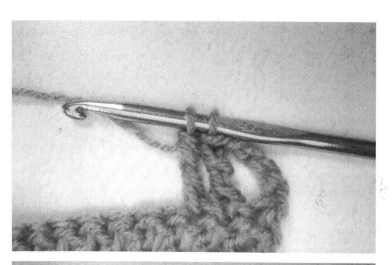

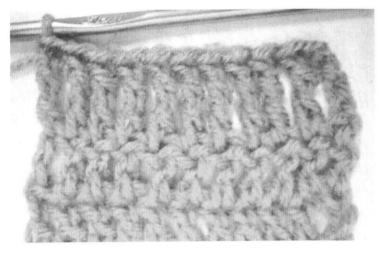

Slip Stitch

In the C2C pattern you will use slip stitches to move the yarn to the proper place when starting a new row of squares. Insert the hook into the next stitch, yarn over, pull through and pull the yarn through the loop on the hook. You do not yarn over again once you pull the yarn through the fabric, but simply pull the yarn through the loop on your hook.

Decrease

A decrease can be done with any of the above basic stitches. What you are doing is crocheting two stitches together. This technique is used to create the valley of a ripple or wave pattern. To crochet a sc2tog (single crochet two together) insert the hook into the first stitch, yarn over, and pull through. Insert the hook into the next stitch, yarn over and pull through. Yarn over and pull through all three loops on the hook crocheting the two single crochet stitches together.

If your pattern calls for a dc2tog you will be crocheting two double crochet stitches together. Start the stitch like normal, yarn over, insert the hook, yarn over and pull through. Yarn over again and insert the hook into the next stitch, yarn over and pull through. Now pull the yarn through all five loops on your hook.

2 stitches worked together for a decrease

2nd st   1st st

Increase

The peaks of a ripple pattern are formed by increases. An increase is simply crocheting more than one stitch into a single stitch. For example if the pattern calls for a three single crochet increase crochet three single crochet stitches into the next stitch. This is true of any stitch you are using. Crochet as many stitches as the pattern calls for into the next stitch. Unlike decreasing you crochet complete stitches in an increase.

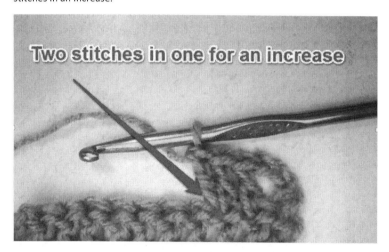

Shell Stiches

Shell stitches, also known as shell clusters, are used in many patterns. They are the basic stitch for Granny Squares and are used in ripple and wave patterns. Like an increase you work more than one stitch into a single stitch. For the basic shell stitch simply crochet three double crochet into one stitch. Some patterns call for more than three double crochet so be sure to check your pattern.

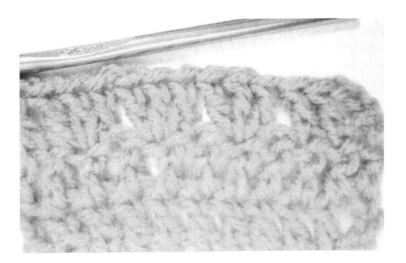

Cluster Stitches

Cluster stitches are similar to shell stitches, but you don't complete the stitches until the very last time you pull the yarn through. To crochet a three double crochet cluster stitch yarn over and insert the hook. Yarn over and pull through two of the loops on the hook. Yarn over and insert the hook into the same stitch and yarn over and pull through. Yarn over and pull through the first two loops on the hook. Yarn over and insert the hook into the same stitch, yarn over and pull through. You will now have four loops on your hook (you will always have one more loop than the number of stitches). Yarn over and pull through all four loops on the hook.

Changing Color

One of the fun things I love about crochet is the chance to work with color. For the beginner changing color may be a bit intimidating, but it is actually very easy. Do not, I say DO NOT, use knots when changing colors. Knots weaken the fabric and they will work out eventually. Instead work the last stitch of the old color until you have two loops left on the hook. Drop the old yarn and pick up the new yarn and draw it through the loops.

On the next stitch catch the old yarn under the new yarn to secure it and pull both colors up snug but not tight. You can use this technique at the end of a row, the end of a round, or in the middle of a row.

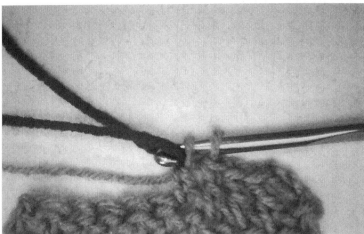

Catch the old yarn under the new color when you finish the stitch.

Continue catching the old and new color tails in the stitches to work them into the fabric and cut down on the tails you have to weave in at the end.

What to do With Ends and Tails

When you crochet your starting chain leave about six inches of yarn to weave in later. Every time you change colors or change yarn leave at least a six inch tail. This will give you enough yarn to weave in the ends correctly so that they do not work their way out over time. Sometimes I will catch the old yarn under the stitches of the row so that I don't have so many ends to weave in. To use this technique insert the hook into the first stitch of the row and place the tail of the new and old yarn on the top of your hook. When you draw the yarn through the stitch catch both tails in the new stitch. Repeat this until you come to the end of the tails. You may have to trim just a bit of the tails sticking out, but this method secures the tails and you won't have to weave them in. This technique works best if you are crocheting in rows or in the round.

Once you complete your project (or while you work on it which is what I like to do so I don't have a million ends to weave in all at once) you will need to weave in the ends and tails. The best way I have found is to use a tapestry needle. Thread the tapestry needle with the tail and weave it in and out of the stitches of the fabric. First go one direction and then turn the fabric and go another direction. This really secures the ends and they won't work out over time. You can change directions as many times as you want depending on how long the tail of yarn is you have to work with.

Corner 2 Corner or C2C Technique

The C2C pattern burst onto the crochet world a few years ago and it has fast become one of the most popular and loved patterns around. This is because it is easy to learn, works up very quickly, and can be used to create many different types of projects. You can use C2C to create afghans, throws, baby blankets, hats, bags, garments, and many home décor projects. Once you get the basic technique down you can experiment with different color combinations and patterns, try different hook sizes, and try different types and weights of yarn.

As the name implies the pattern is worked from one corner to the other. The pattern is worked in a diagonal direction with each row increasing the number of squares until you reach the point at which you want to start to decrease. For a square piece you would start to decrease at the half way point. For a rectangular piece you would stop increasing when you reach the desired width, and start to decrease once you reach the desired length of your project.

Okay now relax, I know that sounds confusing, but we are going to go through how to do all of that in this chapter. Just remember you're not working in actual rows. At first your fabric will form a triangle with each row of blocks increasing.

To start chain six and double crochet into the fourth chain from the hook. These are the first two stitches of the first block. Double crochet into the next two stitches. This is the first block and the starting corner.

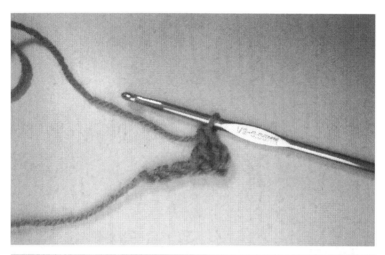

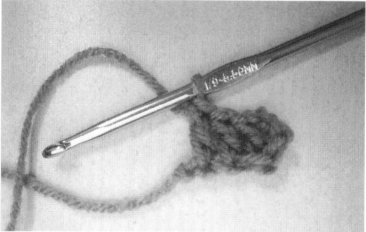

For the next block chain six, work a double crochet into the fourth chain from the hook and into the next two chains.

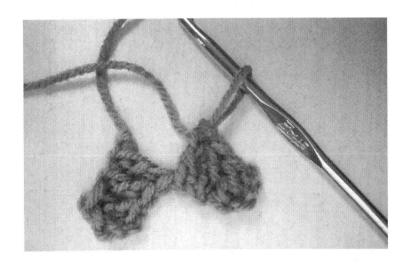

Now slip stitch into the chain three space of the first square and chain three.

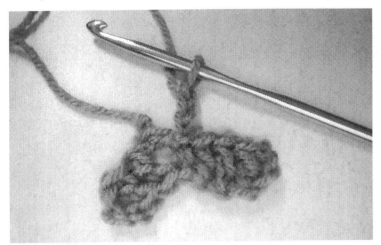

Crochet three double crochet into the chain three space to form the third square and the second square of the second row.

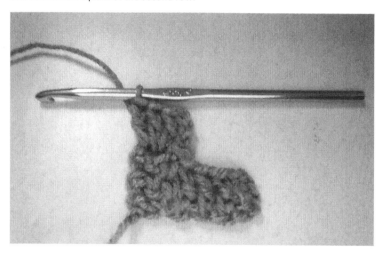

Turn your work and chain six. This is the beginning of the third row. Double crochet into the fourth chain and double crochet into the remaining two chain stitches.

Slip stitch into the next chain three space and chain three. Crochet three double crochet into the chain three space. Slip stitch into the next chain three space and chain three and crochet three double crochet into the chain three space. Repeat this process one more time so that you have three squares In this row.

Turn you work and chain six again and repeat across the row until you come to the last square. Continue to turn your work and chain six until you have reached the width you desire. Once you have your project as wide as you want it, it is time to stop increasing by chaining six on one side of your work.

Once you turn your work you will slip stitch across the edge until you reach the chain three space (four slip stitches). Now chain three and work three double crochet into the chain three space. Crochet across the row and when you reach the end turn your work and chain six on that side to continue to increase only on one side.

If you are making a scarf or rectangular piece you will continue to increase one side until you reach the desired length. If you are making a square stop increasing (chaining six) on both sides once you reach the desired width. Slip stitch and chain three on both sides of the square and this will naturally decrease the rows until you get to the ending corner.

Once you reach the last square slip stitch to the chain three space, double crochet three stitches into the chain three space and break the yarn.

If you want to change colors simply work the last stitch to the last two loops on the hook, grab the new color and pull it through. Chain one and snug up the two colors gently. Don't pull the too tightly or you will make your fabric pucker..

Ripple or Wave Technique

Chances are your grandmother or mother has a ripple afghan or two. This pattern was very popular and now it is experiencing a comeback. The ripple pattern is fun and easy to crochet. There are several variations on the ripple pattern, but they are all based on the peaks and valleys which make up the pattern. When you are working on a ripple pattern make sure your peaks and valleys all line up. This is one way you'll know you're on the right track.

In this chapter we'll cover the basic ripple technique and some fun and cute variations on the pattern. Personally I like to use a variegated yarn and coordinating and contrasting colors to make my projects colorful. How you use color is up to you. You can mix and match solid colors, or use some variegated colors for interest. It's all up to you. You are the artist so don't be afraid to experiment and work with color. Here is the ripple blanket I made as a wedding present recently. I used one variegated yarn and then chose some coordinating colors and threw in dark gray for contrast.

Basic Ripple Pattern

This is a very easy pattern and uses double crochet throughout. First you will need a foundation chain of 148. The first three double crochet count as the first stitch so you will double crochet into the fourth chain from the hook. Start the pattern repeat and double crochet into the next five chain stitches. Now it is time to form the first valley: double crochet two together in the next two chain stitches (dc2tog). Double crochet two together in the next two stitches again. This forms the valley of the ripple. Double crochet into the next five chain stitches. Now you will crochet two double crochet into the next stitch. Crochet two double crochet into the next stitch again. This forms the peak of the ripple pattern. This is the end of the pattern repeat. Work nine more pattern repeats across the first row.

Turn your work and chain three. Double crochet into the first double crochet and start the pattern repeat. Crochet a double crochet into the next five stitches. Now you are at a valley so you need to work two double crochet together into the next two stitches twice. Double crochet into the next five stitches up to the peak of the ripple pattern. Crochet two double crochet into the next stitch twice. This forms the peak and is the end of the pattern repeat. Repeat this pattern seven times and then crochet a double crochet into the next five stitches, double crochet two together twice, crochet five double crochet into the next five stitches, crochet two double crochet into the last stitch and turn your work.

Repeat these two rows until you have the desired length. The pattern calls for 75 rows in total. The pattern also calls for color changes at various intervals. So remember to use the color change technique we covered in the first chapter of this book. (Work the last stitch of the old color until you have two loops on your hook and then pull the new color through.)

Skipped Stitch Variation Ripple Pattern

This variation is similar to the basic pattern, but instead of crocheting two stitches together to form the valleys of the ripple you skip stitches, and the peaks you double crochet, chain one, double crochet. The skipped stitches and chain one create a pretty eyelet effect.

To begin chain 131. Crochet a double crochet into the fifth chain from the hook. This counts as one double crochet and a chain one. Work a double crochet into the next 10 stitches. Double crochet, chain one, double crochet all into the next stitch. Double crochet into the next 11 chains, skip two chains and begin pattern repeat. Double crochet into the next 11 stitches, double crochet, chain one, double crochet all into the next stitch. Double crochet into the next 11 stitches, skip the next two stitches and end the pattern repeat. Crochet the pattern repeat four more times and end with a double crochet into the last chain stitch. You should have five peaks across row one.

Turn your work and chain three. This counts as the first double crochet and skip the first two stitches. Being pattern repeat and double crochet into the next 11 stitches. Double crochet, chain one, double crochet into the next chain one space. Double crochet into the next 11 stitches, skip two stitches and end pattern repeat. Crochet the pattern repeat five times ending with a skip one double crochet and a double crochet stitch into the third turning chain.

Repeat these two rows until you have the desired length. The pattern calls for a total of 81 rows and side edging for the throw. To work the edging hold the right side facing you and join the first color into a corner and chain two. This counts as the first half double crochet. Crochet a half double crochet into the same stitch and across the side of the throw. End with two half double crochet into the last stitch at the end of side one. Fasten off first color.

Join second color at a corner and chain three. Work a double crochet into the same stitch and one double crochet into each half double crochet across the throw ending with two double crochet into the last half double crochet along the edge. Fasten off second color.

Join third color into a corner and chain two. Crochet a half double crochet into the same stitch and into each double crochet across the edge ending with two half double crochet into the last stitch. Fasten off third color.

Turn the throw and work the edging across the opposite side with the right side facing you.

Lots of Options

The ripple pattern is very versatile. You can use many colors or use long strand variegated yarn to get a gradual color change in the pattern. There are lots of projects you can use this pattern for, so don't think you just have to make blankets, afghans, and throws. You can crochet up creative bags, scarves, hats, and home décor items using the ripple technique.

Crochet Resources

There are lots of great resources you can find at stores and online. In this chapter, I will share some of the best resources I've found online to help you expand your skills and find free patterns. There are thousands of free patterns and just as many patterns you can find for sale online and off. The major yarn manufacturers such as Red Heart, Lion Brand, the Caron family have free patterns and learning resource centers on their sites for you check out. Here are just a few of my favorite sites for you to explore.

Red Heart
http://redheart.com
Red Heart sponsors this free site where you can find hundreds of free patterns. You can shop for yarn and supplies in their online store and get everything you need for the projects you download. They also have tutorials and a blog to keep up with all the latest crochet and knitting news and trends. Sign up for the free newsletter to get all the latest patterns and deals from Red Heart.

Lion Brand
http://learntocrochet.lionbrand.com/
Lion Brand is another site where you can find free patterns, yarn, and supplies. They have a learning center where you can learn new skills, and you can keep up with trends and news on their blog. They also offer a free newsletter.

Yarnspirations
http://www.yarnspirations.com/
Home to Caron's, Paton's, Lily's Sugar n Cream, and Bernat yarns this site has hundreds of free patterns, yarn, supplies, and inspiration. The site has a really cool tool called The Inspiration Machine which you can use to find patterns at your skill level. You can also use the tool to find patterns for each season, type of project you want to create, and who the project is for. When you register with the site you can create an online yarn stash, save your favorite patterns, and more.

New Stitch a Day
http://newstitchaday.com/
This site has tons of videos and instruction to learn new stitches. Johnny is personable and gives easy to understand tutorials on stitches and techniques for

all levels of crochet artists. Sign up for their free newsletter and get tutorials delivered to your inbox each day or once a week. The also host live events, contests and giveaways, and discounts for yarn and supplies. Be sure to check out the Video Stitchionary to learn new stitches and brush up on old favorites.

The Crochet Crowd
http://thecrochetcrowd.com/
There is so much free information on this site and a real sense of community. Their YouTube channel is chock full of free tutorials from absolute beginner to advanced techniques. Be sure to follow them on Facebook and check out their challenges. Mikey, Cathy, and Diva Dan offer up humor, thoughtful insights, and plenty of great information on this site. Sign up for their weekly newsletter to keep up to date on all that is going on there.

All Free Crochet
http://www.allfreecrochet.com/Tutorials
I get SO many of my free patterns from this site. There are hundreds if not thousands of free patterns for every level of skill. Sign up for their newsletters and be sure to visit their sister sites for even more free patterns.

All Free Crochet Afghan Patterns
http://www.allfreecrochetafghanpatterns.com/
This is the site where you will find virtually any afghan or throw pattern for free. Patterns range from beginner to advanced and are for the entire family.

Petals to Picots
http://www.petalstopicots.com/
This site has some of the most creative and beautiful patterns which are offered up for free. I have to say I am very impressed with the patterns she shares on her site. Be sure to sign up for her free newsletter and blog to find out what new creations she is offering up.

The Crochet Spot
http://www.crochetspot.com/
This is a great blog full of instructions, illustrations (including left handed instructions), patterns, and information about crocheting for charity. Rachel also

designs patterns you can purchase on her site, and if you sign up for Premium Pattern Membership you can download all of her new patterns each month for no charge.

Crochet N Crafts
http://crochetncrafts.com/freecrochetpatterns.html
A great site full of instructions, videos, free patterns, and patterns you can purchase. There are patterns for all sorts of projects on this site, and lots of tutorials for you to learn new stitches and techniques.

Tapestry Crochet Blog
http://www.tapestrycrochet.com/blog/?cat=18
Carol Ventura has a blog dedicated to the art of flat tapestry crochet. You will find her worldwide adventures finding materials and other loves of this art, and lots of tutorials, patterns, tips, and tricks. You will be amazed at the beautiful creations she creates, and the stunning creations the artists she features on her blog create with this type of crochet.

Crochet Kittens
http://crochetkitten.blogspot.com/
This is another great blog to visit for tutorials, patterns, and lots of information about the art of crochet. Find out how to use your scraps to crochet things for cats in rescue shelters. The Cuddles for Kittens program on her blog gives you a free pattern for a cuddle mat and a cuddle bed you can donate to a local shelter for lonely kitties waiting to be adopted.

Ravelry
https://www.ravelry.com/account/login
Ravelry is a free crochet and knitting community. Here you can meet other hookers in the forums, share patterns, show off your works in progress, and shop for yarn and supplies. If you design patterns you can also post them for free or offer them for sale on the site.

Annie's Crafts

http://www.anniescatalog.com/

Annie's is where you can find all sorts of yarn, supplies, patterns, and everything related to yarn and crafts. Not only do they cover crochet, but they also have lots of information and supplies for jewelry making, knitting, plastic canvas, and more crafts. They also have a free newsletter which keeps you informed of all the specials they offer.

Herrschners

http://www.herrschners.com/

My mother and grandmother received Herschners' free catalogs and I'd spend hours pouring over the beautiful designs and yarn they offered. The quality of their products and patterns is still just as good as it always was and is one of the reasons this is one of my favorite craft sites around.

Mary Maxim

http://www.marymaxim.com/

This is another catalog my mother and grandmother received and I really enjoyed looking at when I was growing up. Their online site is easy to use and they have just about anything you'd need for needle arts and many other crafts.

Videos to Help You Learn and Refresh Your Skills

I find videos wonderful learning tools. I still refer back to them to brush up my skills and I'm always on the lookout for new skills. In this section I am going to share links to videos I think will be helpful to learn not only the techniques in this book, but for crochet in general.

Crochet Exercises: How to Start Crocheting
https://www.youtube.com/playlist?list=PL7E4505A2C54EA604
This is The Crochet Crowd's six part series on the basics of crochet. You can watch and crochet along with Mikey to practice your skills.

The Crochet Crowd Channel Beginner Tutorials
https://www.youtube.com/channel/UCkyBnsdTCZ0DMoMdDdbmo8g
Everything you want to know and learn about crochet is found on this channel. This is a complete series of videos which shows you the basics of how to crochet. (I'm sure you'll just love Mikey, he's funny and a great teacher.)

Learn How to Crochet the Single Crochet Stitch
https://www.youtube.com/watch?feature=player_embedded&v=qELeHz5ar9Q
Lion Brand Yarns

How to Single Crochet
https://www.youtube.com/watch?v=YOlQXn8JWWM&index=4&list=PL69F5A7FE3F95232F
The Crochet Crowd

Learn How to Crochet the Double Crochet Stitch
https://www.youtube.com/watch?v=yB-E6GS84pk
Lion Brand Yarns

How to Double Crochet
https://www.youtube.com/watch?v=bGDxroGp0WY&index=6&list=PL69F5A7FE3F95232F
The Crochet Crowd

How to Double Crochet

https://www.youtube.com/watch?v=bGDxroGp0WY&index=6&list=PL69F5A7FE3F95232F
The Crochet Crowd

Learn How to Crochet the Half-Double Crochet Stitch
https://www.youtube.com/watch?feature=player_embedded&v=GtfZMrgYxLc
Lion Brand Yarns

How to Half-Double Crochet
https://www.youtube.com/watch?v=V0XxnXY9UzU&index=5&list=PL69F5A7FE3F95232F
The Crochet Crowd

Learn How to Crochet the Treble (Triple) Crochet Stitch
https://www.youtube.com/watch?feature=player_embedded&v=AkFtj5ZZWcs
Lion Brand Yarns

How to Treble Crochet
https://www.youtube.com/watch?v=gn5dMFUMGXk&index=7&list=PL69F5A7FE3F95232F
The Crochet Crowd

How to Crochet a Shell Stitch
http://newstitchaday.com/shell-stitch/
New Stitch a Day

How to Crochet the Puff Stitch
http://newstitchaday.com/how-to-crochet-the-puff-stitch/
New Stitch a Day

Corner to Corner Afghan
https://www.youtube.com/watch?v=sNrS4s5C8vc
The Crochet Crowd

Crochet Ripple Afghan aka Wave or Ripple
https://www.youtube.com/watch?v=d1AmNif_gYQ
The Crochet Crowd

Learn to Crochet the Basic Ripple Stitch

https://www.youtube.com/watch?v=zCyQgKCi4QY
Knit Picks

Thank you again for purchasing this book on the popular Corner 2 Corner and Ripple techniques. I hope this book has inspired you to create your very own versions of these popular patterns. I have enjoyed writing this book and my goal is for it to help beginners and more advanced crochet artists alike understand and enjoy these techniques. Unless otherwise noted all images in this book are mine and original. Thanks again and take care!

All my best and keep on hooking!

Dorothy

Made in the USA
San Bernardino, CA
10 April 2018